KEEPSAKE CRAFTS
RIBBONS

HILARY MORE

SUNSET PUBLISHING CORPORATION
MENLO PARK, CALIFORNIA

A QUARTO BOOK

First Printing January 1995

Copyright © 1995 Quarto Inc.

Published by Sunset Publishing Corporation,
Menlo Park, CA 94025

ISBN 0-376-04259-1

Library of Congress Catalog Card Number:
94-068059

For more information on Keepsake Crafts
Ribbons or any other Sunset Book,
call 1-800-634-3095.

This book was designed and produced by
Quarto Inc.
The Old Brewery
6 Blundell Street
London N7 9BH

Senior editor Sally MacEachern
Editor Jane Royston
Senior art editor Amanda Bakhtiar
Designer Alyson Kyles
Photographers Chas Wilder, Paul Forrester
Illustrator Elsa Godfrey
Art director Moira Clinch
Editorial director Sophie Collins

Typeset by Poole Typesetting, Bournemouth
Manufactured in Hong Kong by Regent
Publishing Services Ltd
Printed in China by
Leefung-Asco Printers Ltd

CONTENTS

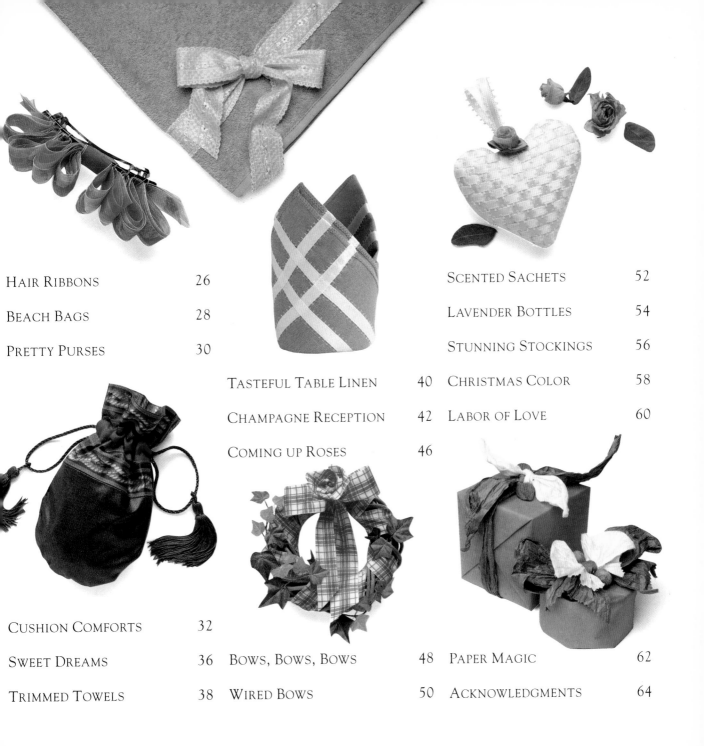

INTRODUCTION

Ribbons have been used through the ages to decorate clothes and furnishings. They are one of the quickest ways of enlivening a garment or household item and, today, with the huge choice of ribbons available, it has become even easier to pick just the right ones for your needs.

With the advent of sophisticated machines and computers, ribbon making and printing has been turned into a fine art, and ribbons come in an impressive range of widths, materials, and designs. Before you begin, survey the different types of ribbons on the market, pick those most suited to your project, and then decide on the pattern and design.

Ribbons can be sewn or glued in place, woven to make a fabric, used as an embroidery thread or simply as a substitute for string. It is important to match your method of attaching the ribbon to the item that you are decorating. Fabric ribbons can be hand- or machine-sewn in place, with their ends cut diagonally or into inverted "V" shapes to prevent fraying. Craft or paper ribbon, on the other hand, will not fray and can be cut, glued, and curled into shape.

As you will see from the ribbon samples shown here, the wonderful array of colors and designs means that it is never hard to find a ribbon that matches your project perfectly.

SINGLE-FACE SATIN RIBBONS

Single-face satin ribbons vary in width. They have one shiny and one dull side, and come in a wide choice of solid colors and printed patterns. Single-face ribbons sometimes also have picot or metallic edges.

DOUBLE-FACE SATIN RIBBONS

Double-face satin ribbons are shiny on both sides and are slightly thicker than the single-face variety. They are available in a good selection of solid colors, sometimes with picot or decorative edges.

POLYESTER RIBBONS

Polyester ribbons are found in an impressive variety of solid colors, printed patterns and finishes (such as crêpe), and they can be combined with metallic strips or woven as tartan plaids.

GROSGRAIN RIBBONS

Grosgrain ribbons are strong and firm with a distinctive crosswise rib. They come in a variety of solid colors, as well as some printed or embroidered stripes and patterns. They can also have satin stripes.

TAFFETA RIBBONS

Flat and matte with a woven design, taffeta ribbons are available in many colors. They may also have a watermarked finish such as moiré, or a picot or metallic edge. Nylon taffeta comes in some wonderful gingham checks.

VELVET RIBBONS

Velvet ribbons have a raised pile and are made of nylon or cotton. They are available as single- or double-face ribbons.

JACQUARD RIBBONS

Jacquard ribbons, woven in a similar fashion to the fabric of the same name, have a slightly raised design. This is often floral, but can also be geometric. Jacquard ribbons also sometimes have a picot edge.

METALLIC RIBBONS

Metallic ribbons are woven from lurex and similar metallic fibers and come in a variety of finishes from sheer to grosgrain.

SHEER RIBBONS

Perfect for making ribbon roses, sheer, light, organdy ribbons can be printed or left plain. Some sheer ribbons have decorative or satin edges, or satin stripes running down the center.

CRAFT RIBBONS
Also known as florists' ribbons, craft ribbons are really strips of fabric which have been given a finish to prevent the edges from fraying when cut. This finish makes them unwashable and therefore unsuitable for some purposes. Craft ribbons come in many solid colors and a huge choice of patterns.

EMBELLISHED RIBBONS
Embellished ribbons have a plain surface that is decorated with beads and sequins, making the ribbons perfect for use on party or bridal wear.

PAPER RIBBONS
Paper ribbons are tightly twisted along their length and can be unwound totally or just in certain sections to create different effects. Fine paper ribbon wound onto spools is also available.

WIRE-EDGED RIBBONS
Wire-edged ribbons have a fine, flexible wire woven along both edges. Once the ribbons are arranged into bows or shapes, they will retain their position indefinitely. One or both of the wires can be removed to create softer effects.

MATERIALS

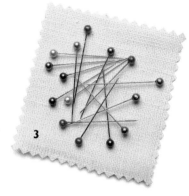

Most of the projects in this book require very little in the way of special materials, but there are a few basic items that you will need. If you do not already have these at home, you will be able to buy them from fabric stores, notions departments, or craft suppliers. For most of the projects, the important point is to choose the materials to match the ribbons you are using. When using adhesives and interfacing, bear in mind the use that the finished item will undergo; for example, you may need to use a stronger glue or a heavier-weight interfacing if the item will receive a reasonable amount of wear and tear

PINS AND NEEDLES

You will need a good selection of pins and needles.

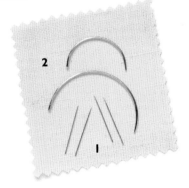

1 Fine quilting needles are extremely useful. **2** Curved needles are ideal for stitching ribbons to awkward shapes. **3** Pins with colored heads are easy to see.

THREADS

Your choice of thread will depend on the type and color of ribbon you are using.

1 Metallic and iridescent threads add texture and interest. **2** Cotton threads can be chosen to match a color scheme.

FUSIBLE INTERFACING

Fusible interfacing is used as a base for ribbon weaving – ribbons can be fused to one side of the interfacing and held in position to form a "fabric." Interfacing is available in light, medium, and heavy weights.

SCISSORS

You will need several types of scissors for working with ribbons.

1 Choose a large pair of sharp scissors for general cutting purposes, such as cutting out paper ribbon, patterns, and fine wires when making ribbon roses (see page 10).

2 A small pair of scissors with sharp points is vital for cutting out small pieces and intricate corners.

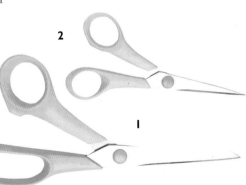

Roses & Rosettes

Ribbon roses look marvelous, whether grouped together in a vase or used with table decorations or on gift wrap the possibilities are endless. The finished result will depend to a great extent on the type of ribbon that you use. Try sheer ribbon for tight, well-formed rosebuds, or double-face satin ribbon for a looser interpretation. Roses can also be created from wire-edged ribbon.

Ribbon rosettes can be made from almost any type of ribbon, as they are simply gathered along one ribbon edge and pulled up into shape. To create a pompon, glue two rosettes back to back on a length of ribbon sandwich style.

RIBBON ROSE ON A STEM

For each rose you will need 29½ inches of 1½-inch-wide sheer ribbon, 20 inches of craft wire, and one stem wire with green tape to cover the stem.

1 Bend over the top of the stem wire to form a loop, and hold the craft wire at the base of the loop. Lay the end of the ribbon over the loop and wrap it with craft wire to secure it.

2 Bring the ribbon up and wrap it around the stem two or three times to create the center of the rose.

3 Begin folding the ribbon away from the center and diagonally forward, catching it at the base each time with the craft wire. At first, fold the ribbon only slightly and wrap tightly, but then, as you work, fold more deeply and ease in more ribbon with each fold to open out the flower.

4 When the rose is the desired size, bring the end of the ribbon down to the base of the flower, and bind with wire to secure. Position the end of the stem binding tape directly under the rose. Bind the stem, securing the tape at the base with adhesive.

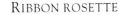

WIRE-EDGED RIBBON ROSE

For a large rose, cut a 42-inch length of wired ribbon.

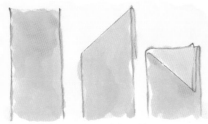

I Fold the cut edge of the ribbon away from you at an angle of 45°. Now fold the ribbon horizontally toward you, keeping the edges even.

2 Continue to fold, making sure that you always fold away from you at a 45° angle

and that when you fold toward you, you pull the front flap forward to make a square as shown above.

3 As you fold, try to pull the outside edge of the ribbon slightly tighter than the inner edge.

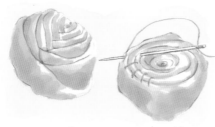

4 When you reach the end of your ribbon, use your fingers to open out the center of the rose into a rounded flower. Hand sew the ribbon end at the base, and continue stitching as necessary to hold the rose shape.

In order to fill the gap left underneath, push a small piece of cotton ball up into the back of the rose to hold the shape. Oversew the edges to keep the cotton ball in place.

RIBBON ROSETTE

Take a piece of ribbon approximately 20 inches in length. Beginning with a knot, run a line of gathering stitches along one straight edge of the ribbon. Pull up the thread to form the rosette, and fasten it securely.

POMPONS

To make a pompon, gather two rosettes and glue them together, back to back (see page 46).

RIBBON WEAVING

Ribbon weaving is similar to traditional weaving, but uses lengths of ribbon instead of yarn. It provides a firm, beautifully textured fabric from which all sorts of different items can be cut and sewn. The easiest way to weave ribbons is over a background of fusible interfacing. Once the ribbons are all in place, simply fuse them to the interfacing with a warm iron.

When weaving with ribbons, the vertical ribbons are the warp threads, while the weft refers to the ribbons that are woven from side to side across the vertical ribbons. The finished pattern can be made simple or complex by using different weaving sequences and also by mixing and matching different ribbon styles and widths in the same piece.

Ribbon weaving is simple to learn. You don't need any complicated equipment, and the finished "fabric" can be used to make pillow covers, bags, place mats, and many other items.

PLAIN WEAVE

Use satin-edged ⅜-inch-wide grosgrain ribbon in two colors.

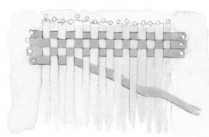

Lay the ribbons of one color out flat, side by side vertically. Working with the other color, lay the ribbons horizontally, weaving the first row under one, over one, and so on, to the end of the row. In the second row, weave the ribbon first over one, then under one, and so on, to the end of the row. The result will be smooth, plain-woven ribbon fabric.

PLAIN WEAVE USING THREE COLORS

By mixing together two different ribbon widths – ⅜ inch and ¼ inch – and three different colors, you will achieve a totally different effect.

Use the same plain-weave method described at left, weaving the horizontal ribbons alternately over and under the vertically positioned ribbons.

TUMBLING-BLOCKS WEAVE

Team up two different pinks, both ¼-inch-wide, with a ⅝- inch-wide cream ribbon to re-create this typical patchwork design.

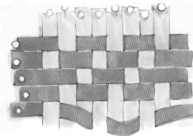

1 Lay out the vertical ribbons, and weave the horizontal ribbons through them. In the first row, work over one, under one, over two, under one, over two, and so on, to the end of the row. In the second row, work under one, over two, under one, over two, and so on, to the end; and in the third row work over two, under one, over two, under one and so on.

DIAGONAL WEAVE

Use a mix of three different-colored ribbons for this diagonal weave – combine a plain ⅞-inch-wide satin ribbon with two ⅞-inch-wide satin-edged grosgrain ribbons.

Lay out all the ribbons of one color vertically as before. For the first horizontal row, weave a ribbon of the second color under one, over two, under two, over two, and so on, to the end of the row. In the second horizontal row, weave a ribbon of the third color under one, over two, under two, over two to the end. Weave the third row over two, under two, over two to the end. In the fourth row, work over one, under two to the end. Repeat these rows to form the diagonal effect.

2 Finally, thread the ⅝ -inch cream ribbon diagonally to create the pattern.

CLASSIC CARDIGAN

Extra-wide patterned ribbon is ideal for decorating a plain knitted sweater to give it a new lease on life and a totally different look.

Transform a plain, long-line cardigan with ribbon to make an interesting and unusual addition to your wardrobe. You could either update a favorite old sweater or begin with a new one. Adding ribbon is an ideal way to liven an inexpensive sweater and make you really stand out in a crowd.

The look that you create will depend on your choice of ribbon. Use wide ribbon with a distinctive *haute-couture* pattern such as the one shown here and add it to the front and pockets of the cardigan. Begin by laying one strip centrally down each front from the shoulder seams; allow a little extra ribbon at the top for turning under later. Tuck the bottom ends neatly inside each front pocket.

To hold the ribbon for stitching, cut a piece of fusible interfacing the same length and slightly less than the width of the ribbon. Center the interfacing under each strip and fuse it in place using an iron set on medium. Turn under the ribbon ends in line with the

Strips of ribbon from shoulder to pocket, with ribbon on the pocket tops, completely transforms this basic cardigan.

shoulder seams to finish the top edges, and then hand sew down each side of the ribbon to secure it. Alternatively, work a loose zigzag stitch on a sewing machine. Take care when doing this; knitting is a flexible fabric, and if the stitches are too tight, they will snap or may pull the cardigan. Complete the decoration with a band of ribbon appliqué across the fronts of the pockets.

You could also add ribbon cuffs to your cardigan, or a simple band or bands of ribbon around each sleeve. As a finishing touch, why not change the buttons, too? Since this type of ribbon is extra-wide, you could use it to make a set of matching covered buttons – follow the manufacturer's instructions for these and then sew them down the front of your cardigan in the usual way.

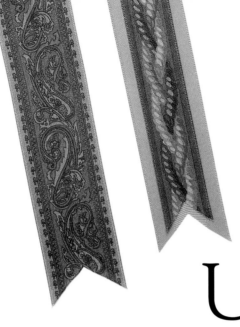

folds where the garment line changes direction. Turn under the raw ends of the ribbon at the top, in line with the shoulder seams, and at the bottom to align with the hem edges.

You can give extra definition to the vest with three pairs of diagonally folded loops of ribbon, evenly spaced on each side of the

UP FRONT

Use ribbon in a

pretty floral design

with coordinating

buttons to decorate

an uninteresting

vest. You could

choose stronger

ribbon colors for an

even more striking

effect.

A simply styled vest never goes out of fashion and makes an indispensable addition to any wardrobe. A vest is neat enough just to wear over a shirt, perhaps in combination with a chic tailored skirt or a pair of slacks, or it can be slipped under a jacket or a heavy, swirling poncho for a "layered" fashion look that is also very warm!

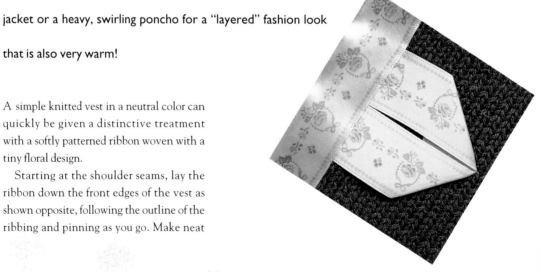

A simple knitted vest in a neutral color can quickly be given a distinctive treatment with a softly patterned ribbon woven with a tiny floral design.

Starting at the shoulder seams, lay the ribbon down the front edges of the vest as shown opposite, following the outline of the ribbing and pinning as you go. Make neat

ribbing. Fold and press each piece of ribbon to provide a pointed edge, and tuck the opposite ends under the vertical ribbons.

Hand sew all the ribbons in place with invisible stitches around the edges, being careful to let the knitted fabric move under the appliqué. The buttons on the vest may now look out of place against the new arrangement, so swap them for pretty buttons that echo the floral feel of the ribbon, and you will be ready to go!

This type of ribbon decoration need not be restricted simply to vests. A collarless jacket would also lend itself beautifully to this treatment, and you could even add a band of the same ribbon to a hat or blouse to create a really spectacular "special-occasion" outfit.

Even when the vest is worn under a jacket or coat, the ribbon will highlight its outline and provide a splash of color.

SNAPPY DRESSER

What could be more appealing than this colorful plaid vest? It would give any plain outfit a lift and could

be worn during the day as a casual accessory or over a simple black evening dress to provide a dramatic

splash. Or add a matching bow tie to create a coordinated look.

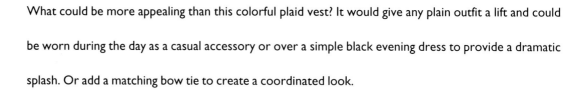

Choose a dressmaking pattern for a plain vest, and cut out the two front sections from fusible interfacing. Cut out the front and back lining, and the back section, from fabric – you could select one of the ribbon colors or stay with a more conventional black-satin lining.

Lay out the interfacing fronts, side by side, with the shiny (fusible) side upward. Take four tartan ribbons – three of ⅞-inch width and one of 3-inch width, and cut and place them at random over both fronts. Place the widest ribbon in position first, and then add the narrower ones haphazardly all around.

Adjust the ribbons until the arrangement looks good across both fronts, and pin to hold them in place. Carefully fuse the ribbons to the interfacing, using an iron on a medium setting, and

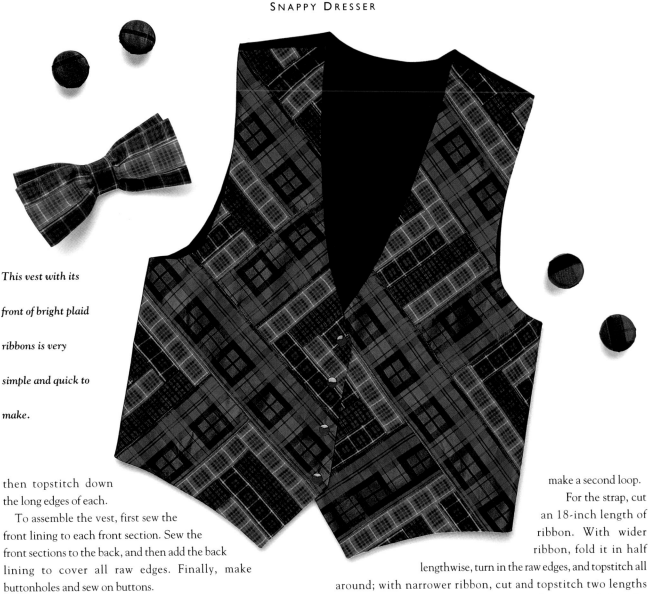

This vest with its front of bright plaid ribbons is very simple and quick to make.

then topstitch down the long edges of each.

To assemble the vest, first sew the front lining to each front section. Sew the front sections to the back, and then add the back lining to cover all raw edges. Finally, make buttonholes and sew on buttons.

To make a bow tie, cut a piece of fusible interfacing 14 inches long by the width of the ribbon or ribbons. Fuse the ribbons to the interfacing. With right sides facing, fold in the short ends to meet in the center. Stitch the sides and turn the bow right side out. Repeat to make a second loop.

For the strap, cut an 18-inch length of ribbon. With wider ribbon, fold it in half lengthwise, turn in the raw edges, and topstitch all around; with narrower ribbon, cut and topstitch two lengths together, tucking in the raw ends. Lay out the strap, and place the two bows, right side out, centrally on top of it. Bind the center with a short strip of ribbon, and add a hook and eye to the ends of the strap to complete.

Diagonal lengths of floral ribbon decorate the bodice of this white dotted-swiss dress. Cut out the front and back bodice pieces from fusible interfacing, using a simple dressmaking pattern if you wish.

Lay the pieces out flat, with the shiny side up. Lay ½-inch wide embossed ribbons diagonally across the interfacing, with the edges butting together. Pin and fuse the ribbons in place. The ribbons are narrow, so there is no need to stitch them in place, but make sure that you have pressed them firmly. Stitch a fabric lining to the inside of the bodice. Leave an opening in the back for the head.

Narrow ribbon embossed with tiny flower patterns is ideal for a little girl's party dress.

LITTLE MISS PRETTY

Party dresses must be pretty and feminine, and adding ribbon is the perfect way to decorate a plain dress or one that needs a new look. This practical pinafore is very quick to make and slips over a dress, creating a unique party outfit.

Cut out the skirt from fabric. To finish the side and hem edges quickly, turn the edges to the right side, lay a harmonizing ribbon against the outer edge to cover the raw fabric edges, and topstitch in place. Add a ribbon tie on each side of the skirt.

Softly gather the top edge of the skirt with running stitches, and sew it to the bodice, inserting lengths of ribbon into the seam at intervals. Make a fastening for the back bodice at the neck edge with a button and loop. Slip the finished pinafore over the child's head and fasten it on each side with the ribbon ties.

The ribboned bodice turns this simple pinafore into a pretty outfit with coordinating ties and edging.

ONE STEP AHEAD

An elegant flower design in cream ribbon looks stunning on a black shoe.

Put your best foot forward with these smart shoe trims. Simple shoes – whether destined for the beach or a party – look wonderful with the addition of ribbons and bows. Ribbon rosettes of all colors and sizes can be quickly made and anchored to the fronts of shoes.

The contrast of cream against black creates the stylish look on the left. Take seventeen 1½-inch lengths of 1¼-inch-wide ribbon, and clip the corners of each length to make a diamond shape. To form the petals, roll each long edge of the diamonds into the center and sew each end together with one or two tiny stitches.

Cut a 1¼-inch diameter cardboard circle, and glue the petals in place around it. Glue a

Give espadrilles a

new lease on life

with pretty rosettes

(below). You could

add ribbon ties, too,

as a special touch.

black button in the center to complete the flower. Make a second flower in the same way, and fasten the cardboard circles to shoe clips.

Transform espadrilles into something unusual with ribbon rosettes (below). Use 3-inch-wide sheer ribbon in the colors of your choice, fold it in half, and then gather it up with running stitch along one edge to make the rosette (see page 11). Bunch the rosettes

together across the fronts of the espadrilles and sew in place. Finally, if you wish, cut two lengths of ¼-inch-wide satin ribbon and sew one to each side of the backs of the espadrilles.

To make the folded-ribbon rosette above, cut twenty-one 3-inch lengths of ⅝-inch-wide bordered ribbon, and a 1¼-inch diameter cardboard circle. Fold and press each length of ribbon in half, and glue one length overlapping the next around the cardboard with the raw edges in the center.

When the rosette is complete, glue a gilt button in the center. Make a second rosette in the same way, and fasten the cardboard circles to shoe clips.

Gold-edged ribbon

topped with a gilt

button creates a

sophisticated look

for shoes (above).

You could use bright

ribbon and buttons

for more casual

shoes.

Grosgrain ribbons in navy and navy-and-white dots make up the elegant trim on the straw hat below. The ribbon here is 1½ inches wide. You will need enough to go around your hat brim with a small overlap, plus approximately 20 inches for the bow.

Stitch the two ribbons for the hat brim together, overlapping the polka dot ribbon slightly to create a different width, and place them around the hat. For the bow, stitch the

RIBBON HAT TRIMS

The stunning hat decoration above is easy to create. First, cut a felt-circle base measuring 2¼ inches in diameter. Cut nine 5½-inch pieces of sheer blue ribbon, press them in half, and stitch them to the felt in a half-fan arrangement.

Cut seven 4-inch pieces of sheer printed ribbon, iron them into petal shapes, and stitch them to the fan. Trim the center with a blue ribbon rose (see page 10). Cut a length of sheer printed ribbon to fit around the hat, plus a small overlap, and sew the decoration over the seam.

Transform your hats with colorful bands and unusual decoration. Combine pretty patterned ribbons with velvet, felt, and straw to give each hat a new image – you could even sew several bands for each hat and change them to match different outfits.

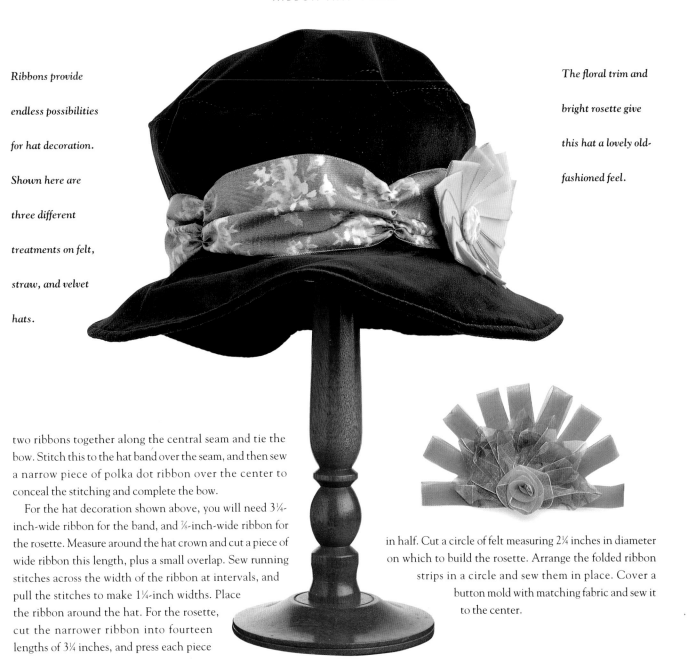

Ribbons provide

endless possibilities

for hat decoration.

Shown here are

three different

treatments on felt,

straw, and velvet

hats.

The floral trim and

bright rosette give

this hat a lovely old-

fashioned feel.

two ribbons together along the central seam and tie the bow. Stitch this to the hat band over the seam, and then sew a narrow piece of polka dot ribbon over the center to conceal the stitching and complete the bow.

For the hat decoration shown above, you will need 3¼-inch-wide ribbon for the band, and ⅞-inch-wide ribbon for the rosette. Measure around the hat crown and cut a piece of wide ribbon this length, plus a small overlap. Sew running stitches across the width of the ribbon at intervals, and pull the stitches to make 1¼-inch widths. Place the ribbon around the hat. For the rosette, cut the narrower ribbon into fourteen lengths of 3¼ inches, and press each piece

in half. Cut a circle of felt measuring 2¼ inches in diameter on which to build the rosette. Arrange the folded ribbon strips in a circle and sew them in place. Cover a button mold with matching fabric and sew it to the center.

HAIR RIBBONS

An elegant barrette of woven ribbons (above), contrasts with a colorful rosette on elastic (below).

A simple but striking ribbon design decorates this hair band.

Ribbons make ideal hair decorations. Instead of using them just to tie up pony tails and bunches, weave them or create rosettes. Attach them to barrettes, bands, and elastic straps to make hair ornaments guaranteed to make heads turn in your direction.

To cover a plain barrette such as the one shown above left, weave together narrow green satin and velvet ribbon. Cut four pieces of satin ribbon, each longer than the barrette. Fasten them on the back, across one narrow end, and bring them around to the front. Secure the velvet ribbon at the back and start wrapping it around the barrette. As you wrap, weave the satin ribbon under and over in a plain weave. Secure the ends as at the start of the barrette.

Double-sided print ribbon was used for the rosette on the left. Cut a 36-inch length and turn under the cut ends, holding them with a zigzag stitch. Fold down one corner to make a point at one end. Sew a line of running stitch down the longer ribbon edge, catching down the folded corner. Gather the ribbon tightly and knot the thread.

26

Coil the ribbon around the pointed end, sewing the layers as you work. Sew the rosette to elastic.

Mix three $\frac{1}{12}$-inch ribbons to form the braided hair band shown on the left. Cut 19-inch lengths of each color, and glue them side by side on the band, starting about ⅛ inch from one end. Wrap the ribbons around the band, keeping them flat, in the correct order and as close together as possible. Glue the ends inside the band ⅛ inch from the end. To highlight the center, make a flat braid the length of the band and tuck the ends into the bound ribbon, three rows from the end on each side. Glue in place.

To make the loopy barrette below, cut five 24-inch lengths of sheer ribbon: two printed, two dark pink, and one green. Layer the five ribbons together, and wire them to the barrette to create eight loops. Spread the ribbons apart to create fullness, and wind a piece of ribbon around the center to complete the "bow."

For the comb on the right, cut two 13¼-inch lengths of 1⅛-inch-wide Jacquard ribbon. Fold each length into a loop and sew the cut ends together. Lay the two loops side by side, with the seams at center back, and gather up the loops on each side of the center. Trim with a sheer ribbon rose (see page 10) and sew to a hair comb.

The "caterpillar" barrette below is easy to make. Cut a sheer ribbon and a narrower Jacquard ribbon three times longer than the barrette. Lay the narrower ribbon centrally over the wider ribbon. Turn under the cut ends and sew a running stitch up the center through both ribbons. Pull the thread to gather the ribbon down the length of the barrette, and place a few stitches at the end to secure the gathers. Glue the ribbons to the barrette.

A double bow and ribbon rose decorate a hair comb (above); and sheer and Jacquard ribbons make an attractive barrette (below).

Pastel-colored ribbons create lavish loops on this barrette.

BEACH BAGS

Pick strong ribbons in primary colors, and use them to create fun beach or shopping bags. You can make your bright new-look carriers as small, as large, or as vibrant as you like!

Woven, sewn, or glued ribbons turn plain bags into colorful accessories.

To make the small purse on the left, cut a piece of fabric 13½ x 6¼ inches. Fold 8¼ inches across the width with right sides together and stitch each side. Turn right side out to form the purse and flap. Cut five lengths of ribbon and stitch them along the flap. Make a shoulder strap from a folded ribbon, and stitch it to each side of the purse. Sew a piece of ribbon inside the flap, and a corresponding piece on the purse to fasten the flap.

For the duffle bag opposite, cut a piece of sturdy fabric 26 x 16½ inches for the bag side. Choose three ribbons, cut each in half, and stitch them along each side edge of the fabric. Fold the fabric and sew the side seam.

Cut an 8-inch-diameter fabric base and stitch this to the side piece. Turn the bag right side out and bind the top edge. Stitch a casing below the ribbons at the top, leaving a gap on each side. Cut two lengths of ⅛-inch-wide ribbon and thread each through the casing. Knot the ends, and pull up the ribbons for ties.

To make the shopping bag, cut two pieces of woven fusible interfacing and backing fabric, each 12½ x 17¼ inches. Lay the interfacing flat, with the shiny side up. Weave ribbons over the interfacing and fuse in place. Fold with right sides together and, leaving the top open, stitch to the backing fabric. Turn right side out, finish the top edge, and add ribbon handles.

PRETTY PURSES

Keep your change or cosmetics in a pretty ribbon bag. Ribbon also makes an ideal decoration on tiny drawstring purses for special evenings. Match the ribbon colors to your favorite outfit, or make several bags for different occasions!

A simple criss-cross pattern looks attractive on this cosmetics bag.

Choose a plain fabric background for this cosmetics bag. Cut out two pieces of fabric measuring 6 x 10½ inches. Topstitch ribbon diagonally in each direction across each piece. Turn under the seam allowance along the top edges, and sew each edge to one side of a zipper. Stitch all around the remaining three sides, trim the edges, and turn the purse right side out through the open zipper.

The little bag on the right is very quick to make. Cut two pieces of fusible interfacing 7½ x 5 inches. On each piece, lay patterned ribbons in bands across the shape, adding a plain extra-wide ribbon at the base. Stitch a casing made from a 1½-inch-wide ribbon to the right side, 2 inches from the top.

Use a small saucer as a template to round off the bottom edges on each piece. Place the right sides together, and

The "fabric" of

these little bags is

made of ribbon, with

tasseled cords to

draw them closed.

stitch all around, leaving the top edge open. Turn under the top edge and stitch a narrow hem. Turn the bag right side out. Thread cord through the casing and add a tassel to each end.

To make the bag on the left, cut a piece of fusible interfacing 15 x 12 inches. Lay it flat with the shiny side up. Lay ⅛-inch-wide patterned ribbons lengthwise over the whole piece and fuse in place. Fold the raw top edges to the outside, and bind with ⅛-inch-wide ribbon. Add a casing of the same ribbon on the right side of the fabric, 3¼ inches from the top edge. Fold the fabric in half with the right sides together and sew a seam. Cut a 4¼-inch-diameter circle of fabric and stitch this into the base. Thread cord through the casing and add a tassel to complete.

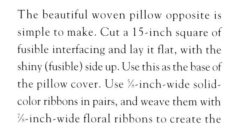

The beautiful woven pillow opposite is simple to make. Cut a 15-inch square of fusible interfacing and lay it flat, with the shiny (fusible) side up. Use this as the base of the pillow cover. Use ⅝-inch-wide solid-color ribbons in pairs, and weave them with ⅞-inch-wide floral ribbons to create the

CUSHION COMFORTS

Your ideas for throw pillows will be endless when you see the vast selection of ribbons with which to make them. The décor of a room will usually dictate the color, but you can still pick your ribbons from many patterned and textured varieties. You could relate a series of pillows, giving each one its own look with a different weave or ribbon arrangement.

Plain and floral ribbons create a lovely effect on the pillow opposite. See pages 12–13 for examples of basic weaves and instructions.

pattern shown here. When the design looks good and is tightly woven, fuse the ribbons in place using a medium-hot iron. To make sure that the ribbons will hold, turn over the interfacing and press it again on the wrong side.

The diagonally woven cover (page 34) is made in the same way as the pillow, but the weave is different. Lay half the ribbons

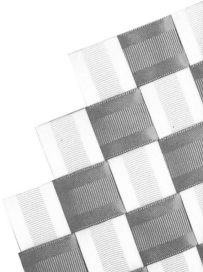

diagonally across the interfacing, then
tightly weave the remaining ribbons
vertically through them. Fuse the ribbons in
position, again pressing from both sides to
achieve a firm fabric.

Overlapping diagonal ribbons
make an attractive design on the
pillow opposite (top). Cut a
15-inch square of fusible
interfacing and lay
it flat, with the
shiny side up. Use a
combination of cream,
rust, and peach ribbons in 1½-
inch, 1¼-inch, and ⅝-inch widths to
make the pattern. Lay the ribbons
diagonally across the interfacing in both
directions, as shown, to create the design.
Fuse the ribbons in place and, to hold them
firmly, topstitch each one along the outer
edges. Add definition to the central pattern
with a border made with the rust-colored
ribbon. Pin this in position, and then
topstitch the edges to hold the ribbon
securely in place.

To create the diagonal design below,
cut a 15-inch square of fusible interfacing

Harmonizing

ribbons woven

diagonally create

the eye-catching

design shown on

the left.

and lay it flat, with the shiny side up. Use 1⅛-inch- and ⅞-inch-wide ribbons in cream and rust, and mix these with a striped ribbon in rust, cream, and green. Simply lay the ribbons side by side diagonally over the interfacing and fuse them in place. Topstitch close to the edge of each ribbon to make sure that they are held firmly in place.

Make each cover in the same way. Cut two back pieces from plain fabric, each measuring 8 x 15 inches. Seam the two back pieces together inserting a zipper. Undo the zipper and pin the back to the front with right sides facing. Stitch all around, taking a ⅝-inch seam allowance. Trim the seams. Turn the cover right side out, and insert a pillow.

The ribbons used here were chosen to suit a color scheme, but select your ribbons to match your own décor.

The elegant pair of

pillows created with

striking designs in

rust, pink, and

cream ribbons.

The ribbon decoration across the corner of the pillowcase on the left is simple but very attractive. Cut ⅜-inch-wide ribbon into five graduating lengths and topstitch them in place diagonally across one corner, leaving evenly spaced gaps between each ribbon and

A simple ribbon design such as the one on the left transforms a plain pillowcase.

SWEET DREAMS

Plain pillowcases look marvelous with decorative additions, and are easy to handle. Match or contrast ribbon colors with pillowcases, or use pretty picot-edged ribbons to provide a delicate touch.

neatly turning under the cut edges. You could add more ribbon rows if you wish, but, unless you sew them by hand rather than machine, these may become awkward to sew as you move away from the open edge of the pillowcase.

To create the design on this cream pillowcase, cut a length of picot-edged dark ribbon, to contrast with the background, and pin it to the open end of your pillowcase, 2 inches from the edge. Stitch the ribbon in place. Next, cut a piece of narrower, cream-colored ribbon into two uneven lengths.

Beginning at the side of the pillowcase, center the shorter length over the wider ribbon, and stitch it in place for approximately 4 inches. At the top, stitch the second length of ribbon centrally over the wider ribbon. Tie the trailing ends of the ribbons into a bow, between the two sewn strips.

For the navy pillowcase, cut one length of decorative ribbon and pin it along the open end of a pillowcase, 4 inches from the edge. Cut short lengths of the same ribbon and pin them diagonally from the pillowcase edge to the ribbon band, as shown. Tuck the inner cut ends under the ribbon band, and turn under the opposite ends in line with the pillowcase edge. Baste and then topstitch the ribbons in place to secure them firmly.

Ribbon tied in a bow gives a feminine look to a cream pillowcase (above), while a geometric pattern suits a navy background.

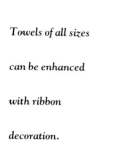

Towels of all sizes

can be enhanced

with ribbon

decoration.

A lace-ribbon

TRIMMED TOWELS

bow gives a pretty

finish to the powder

blue hand towel

shown above.

The pretty lace bow shown above is perfect for a small hand towel. Take a piece of 1½-inch-wide lace ribbon measuring the length of the towel plus about 8 inches for the bow. Cut the ribbon into a short and a longer length. Turning under the cut ends, pin and stitch one piece along the woven border on the towel from the left-hand edge and the other piece from the right-hand edge, leaving 4 inches of each ribbon unstitched. Tie these ends in a bow and catch with a few hand stitches to secure.

Brighten up bath time with beribboned towels. Pastel towels especially benefit from the addition of ornamental bands of ribbons. Use the ribbon shades to tie together an assortment of different-colored towels into one attractive color scheme that suits your décor.

For the zigzag design on the right, cut a length of ⅛-inch-wide picot-edged ribbon and fold it in a zigzag pattern along the woven border of the towel. Turn under the cut ends to finish, and baste and topstitch in place.

To create the stripes below, cut two lengths of ⅛-inch-wide picot-edged ribbon and baste one piece to each side of a lace ribbon. Stitch this in place along the woven towel border, turning under the cut ends to finish.

For the pink-on-pink design on the pink towel, wrap ⅛-inch-wide picot-edged ribbon around 1⅛-inch-wide eyelet ribbon to form a diagonal pattern. Stitch this in position. Stitch the ribbon along the woven border of the towel, turning under the cut ends to finish them.

Ribbons are perfect

for coordinating

bathroom

accessories, as

this small set of

pastel towels shows.

*Add sophistication
to your table with
crisp ribbon-
trimmed napkins
such as the one
shown below.*

TASTEFUL TABLE LINEN

Plain ribbons look beautiful on table linens. Make a set of napkins with a matching tablecloth, or use your ingenuity to decorate the edges of each napkin with a different design. Weave the ribbons together at the corners or create a single striking motif – the choice is yours.

The possibilities for decorating napkins with ribbons are almost limitless. Shown on the left and opposite are two examples which are easy to make, but look stunning. For the napkin on the left, cut and pin a length of ⅜-inch-wide picot-edged ribbon to fit along each side, 1½ inches inside the outer edge. Pin a second length of ribbon ¼ inch inside the first ribbon. Weave the ribbons at the corners where they cross. Baste and topstitch the ribbons in place, stitching along both edges for a secure finish that will withstand laundering.

To make the design shown opposite, cut a length of 1½-inch-wide ribbon to fit along three sides of the napkin. Pin the ribbon in place, mitering the corners neatly and concealing the cut edges. Baste and then topstitch the ribbon, stitching along both edges.

Add interest to a tablecloth, such as the one on the right, by

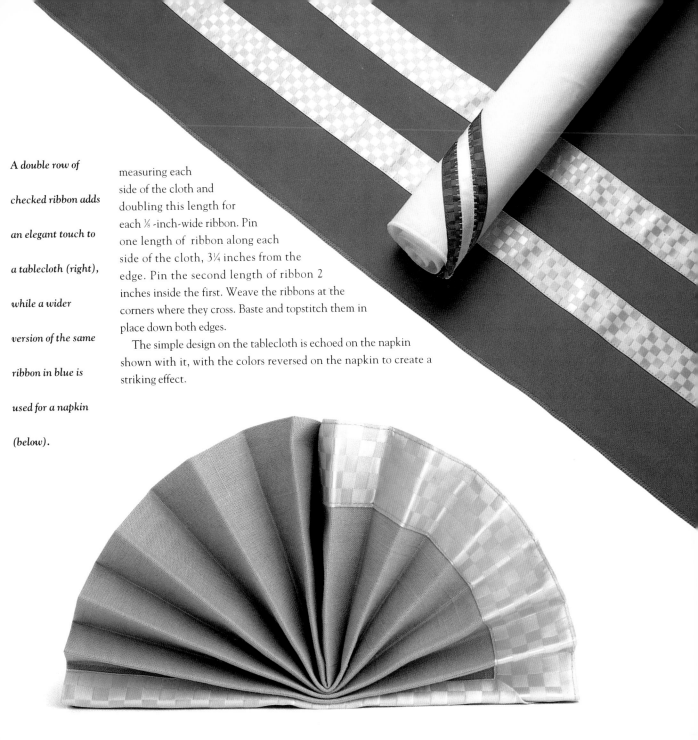

A double row of checked ribbon adds an elegant touch to a tablecloth (right), while a wider version of the same ribbon in blue is used for a napkin (below).

measuring each side of the cloth and doubling this length for each ⅛-inch-wide ribbon. Pin one length of ribbon along each side of the cloth, 3¼ inches from the edge. Pin the second length of ribbon 2 inches inside the first. Weave the ribbons at the corners where they cross. Baste and topstitch them in place down both edges.

The simple design on the tablecloth is echoed on the napkin shown with it, with the colors reversed on the napkin to create a striking effect.

The dainty bonbonnière shown on the left would look attractive on any table. Cut an 11-inch square of fine net and topstitch a narrow picot-edged ribbon around the outer edge. Place a few candied almonds in the center and gather the net with two lengths of ribbon – one pink, one white – and tie into a bow. Trim the ribbon ends diagonally.

A pretty pink-and-white color scheme has been used for the stunning display opposite.

Candied almonds in a beribboned bonbonnière (above) make a charming little gift for wedding guests.

CHAMPAGNE RECEPTION

For the stunning tablecloth opposite, measure the table top and add 32 inches to this diameter for an overhang. Cut a circle of plain white cotton fabric to this size. Finish the edge and topstitch a length of narrow picot-edged ribbon around it.

Next, divide the cloth into six equal sections, and, at each of these points, work two rows of gathering stitches up to the table edge. Pull up the cloth and tie the threads. Tie lengths of wire-edged ribbon into extravagant bows, and hand sew one at each gather.

Weave a magical spell around a wedding reception with beautiful ribbons. Combine embroidered and sheer ribbons to make pretty candle holders, napkin rings, and a ring pillow, (see pages 44–45.) Tie lavish bows to a ruched tablecloth to create a spectacular table setting.

To make the delicate ring pillow below, cut two pieces of white cotton fabric, each 9 inches square. On the front piece, add a border of 1½-inch-wide embroidered ribbon ⅝ inch from the outer edge. Miter the corners neatly to fit. Add a second border of 1¼-inch-wide eyelet ribbon inside the first, this time overlapping the edges at the corners to form a neat edge. Topstitch both ribbons in place.

Gather a sheer white-edged ribbon twice the length of the outer edge.

Spacing the gathers evenly, pin and baste this around the outer edge. With right sides facing, pin and stitch the back to the front, leaving an opening in one side. Trim and turn the cover right side out, insert filling and overcast the opening. Tie a bow of picot-edged ribbon at each corner. Add a slightly larger one in the center to hold the rings. Then, sew them in place.

To make the unusual candle holder opposite, first cut a 6-inch-diameter cardboard circle and glue a paper doily over the top. For the outer edge, cut 8-inch lengths of white embroidered 1⅝-inch-wide ribbon. Fold each length into a petal shape, and glue the petals around the circle in pairs, spacing them evenly. Glue two 8-inch loops of extra-wide sheer ribbon in between each pair.

For the second layer, make five large flowers from plain sheer ribbon. To do this, fold a long length of extra-wide sheer ribbon into petals, layering them one on top of the other to form the flower. Space the flowers evenly around the cardboard and glue them in place, adding a large "pearl" in the center of each. Leave the center of the arrangement free for the candle holder of your choice.

This exquisite ring pillow (below left) has embroidered ribbon borders, ribbons at the center and corners, and a sheer edging ribbon.

Make the matching napkin ring by placing interfacing between two 9-inch lengths of embroidered ribbon and topstitching the layers together around the outer edges. Sew into a ring. Take two short pieces of embroidered ribbon and form each into a diamond shape by folding the inner edges together. Attach the ends to the ring to form a bow shape. Make a sheer flower, with a pearl center, following the instructions given for the candle holder, and then hand sew the flower to the napkin ring to cover the seams.

This delicate napkin ring (above) matches the candle holder beautifully to make a perfect table setting.

The sheer cream ribbon used for this candle holder looks beautiful in the glow of the candle flame.

The photograph frame opposite is easy to make. First, cover your chosen frame with velvet. Dark green has been used here to match the other accessories, but you could of course use any color velvet. Make two pale pink, one dark pink, and one cream rose from satin ribbon, and arrange them on the frame. Wrap the stems together, finishing with a dark pink bow and adding leaves.

The first step in making the coat-hanger shown above is to wrap the hook with cream ribbon. Next, measure the length of the hanger and double this length; then measure around the hanger and add a ⅜-inch seam allowance. Cut a piece of green velvet to these measurements. Fold the velvet around the hanger, turn in the allowance, and pin the folded edges together. Gather the folded edge from each side and sew the ends.

Using two shades of pink ribbon, make two rosettes (see page 11) and three roses (see page 10) from each. Tie a length of cream ribbon around the hook so that the ends hang down, and glue two rosettes back to back around each end. Stitch the 6 roses around the hook.

COMING UP ROSES

Try making this colorful set of coordinating accessories –

combining luxurious velvet fabric with cream and pink rosebuds

and rosettes – for your bedroom. These attractive pieces would make wonderful

gifts too. Each one can easily be made in an evening.

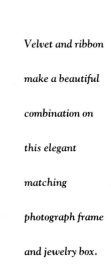

The extravagant

coathanger opposite

will add luxury to

any wardrobe and is

fit for your most

elegant clothes.

Glue the arrangement to one corner of the frame, as shown.

Lavish ribbon rosettes look wonderful on the lid of a velvet-covered jewelry box (below). If you do not already have a box of this type, you will be able to buy one fairly inexpensively. Or you could make your own by lining and covering a suitable box with velvet. To add the lid decoration, make five cream, five pale pink, and five dark pink rosettes. Glue them randomly on the box lid, and add a few folded ribbon leaves between the flower shapes to finish.

Velvet and ribbon

make a beautiful

combination on

this elegant

matching

photograph frame

and jewelry box.

BOWS, BOWS, BOWS

Ribbon can be stiffened and shaped with special solutions or diluted craft glue. Arrange the ribbons, then simply paint over both sides with the glue mixture. The ribbon will stiffen, remain in the fixed position and gain a shiny surface that creates an attractive effect.

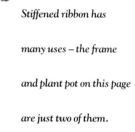

Stiffened ribbon has many uses – the frame and plant pot on this page are just two of them.

Use a colored photograph mat for the frame shown on the opposite page. Cut a length of reversible green-and-red gold-edged ribbon, and tie a bow in the center. Coat both sides of the ribbon with diluted adhesive, and then glue the bow to the top of the mat. Glue the ribbon ends to each side of the frame in loops, using pins to hold them until they are completely dry.

Woven plant pots look very attractive with a ribbon trim. To make the type shown at left, cut a piece of extra-wide ribbon one-and-a-half times the circumference of the pot top. Fold it in half widthwise over the pot edge, pin and sew. Tie a large bow and sew it to the basket, over the ribbon seam. Coat both the ribbon edge and the bow with diluted adhesive and let it dry.

The decoration on the cane wreath above is simple, but looks very effective. Wrap the wreath with red-and-white gingham ribbon, fastening it at the top. Cut a length of the same ribbon, tie it into a bow, and attach it to the top of the wreath. Cut the ribbon ends diagonally, letting them trail. Make a ribbon rose and fasten it over the bow. Paint the ribbons with diluted adhesive and let them

Red-and-white

gingham ribbon tied

in an extravagant

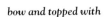

bow and topped with

a rose gives this

wreath a lovely

country feel.

dry; then, intertwine greenery or dried flowers as desired.

The little basket below uses the same ribbon as the wreath. Wrap the basket handle and tie lengths of ribbon into bows on each side. Cut the ends diagonally. Stiffen the ribbon with diluted adhesive and let it dry thoroughly.

The same gingham

ribbon transforms

the woven basket

below. A wide floral

ribbon would also

look pretty.

Luxurious floral-and-gold ribbon creates a stunning arrangement.

Poppy seedheads sprayed with gold complete the rich effect.

Dried hydrangea and gold-sprayed popp seedheads were chosen to complement the beautiful gold-backed floral ribbon in the nosegay at left. To make it, first wrap the plant stems with wire, and then make a four loop bow. Begin by forming two loops in conventional bow shape, finishing with the remaining length of ribbon on the top to make a "cross" in the center. (Don't worry about the neatness of the bows at this stage as these can be adjusted at the end.)

Hold the loops in place with your thumb and index finger. Make a third and fourth loop in the same way, bringing the end of the ribbon over the middle of the bow once again to make a second cross, and leaving one long end to trail. Cut the ribbon ends on a slant to finish them. Ease the bow into

WIRED BOWS

A shiny, patterned ribbon adorns an eye-catching wreath (right).

Wire-edged ribbon is wonderful for creating lavish bows. It is easy to mold and retains its shape indefinitely. You can use wire-edged ribbon throughout a design, or you could remove part of the wire and make trailing streamers to complement crisp wired bows.

shape so that the loops cover the central binding wire. Bind the center of the bow with fine wire, and then pin a strip of ribbon over it to resemble a self-tie.

The small bouquet on this page looks beautiful with its delicate bow of gold-edged cream ribbon. To make it, first bind together your chosen flower stems with wire. Create the six-loop bow by following the previous instructions for a four-loop bow, adding the fifth and sixth loops in the same way.

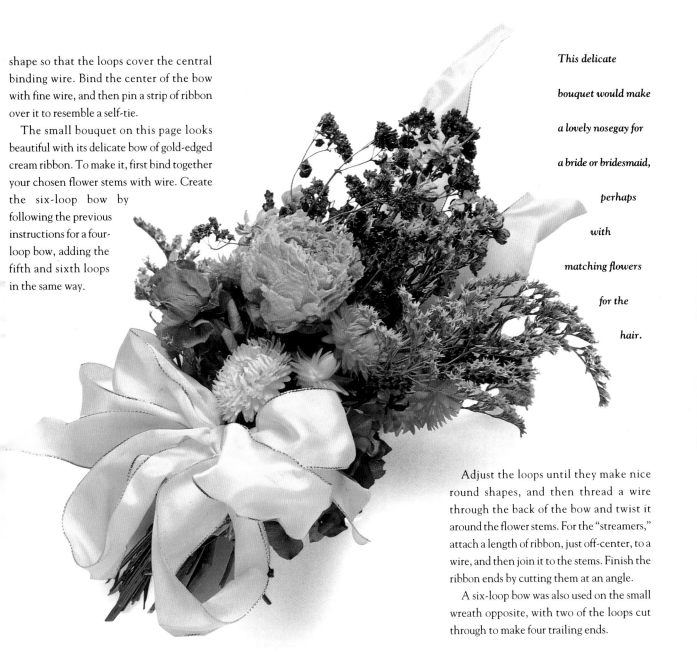

This delicate bouquet would make a lovely nosegay for a bride or bridesmaid, perhaps with matching flowers for the hair.

Adjust the loops until they make nice round shapes, and then thread a wire through the back of the bow and twist it around the flower stems. For the "streamers," attach a length of ribbon, just off-center, to a wire, and then join it to the stems. Finish the ribbon ends by cutting them at an angle.

A six-loop bow was also used on the small wreath opposite, with two of the loops cut through to make four trailing ends.

Make the little heart sachet on the left by cutting picot-edged ribbon in two colors into 5-inch lengths. Cut a 5-inch square of fusible interfacing, and lay this shiny side up. Weave the ribbons to form a fabric (see pages 12–13), and fuse them in place. Cut out a heart shape from this ribbon fabric, and also from cheesecloth or thin cotton lining fabric. Place the fabrics right sides together, and pin and stitch all around, leaving an opening. Trim the

SCENTED SACHETS

Ribbons add the perfect touch to tiny potpourri sachets. Cheesecloth allows the scent to escape.

Pretty pastel sachets are perfect to slip between your clothes to keep them smelling sweet. Fill each one with your favorite potpourri to create a lovely fragrance.

Picot-edged ribbons in pink and cream are perfect for a little sachet (above).

seam and turn the fabric right side out. Fill the heart with potpourri and overcast the opening. Sew on ribbon loops to hang up the heart, and add a small ribbon rose to complete.

The three sachets opposite are easy to make. For the "sack" shape, cut two pieces of cheesecloth 4 x 13¼ inches and stitch floral picot-edged ribbon diagonally across the two bottom corners on each piece of cheesecloth. Stitch the two pieces together on three sides, leaving the fourth (short) side open. Trim the seams and turn right side out. Fold down ¼ inch around the top edge and stitch matching ribbon around the top to cover this cut edge. Fill the bag with potpourri and tie it up with ribbon.

For the pillow, cut a piece of fusible interfacing measuring 4½ x 5½ inches. Cut two different ribbons into 4-inch lengths. Overlapping the edges and alternating the ribbons, fuse them to the interfacing. With right sides together, stitch the ribbon fabric to cheesecloth backing fabric, leaving an opening. Trim the seam, turn and fill with potpourri. Slipstitch the opening.

To make the parcel, cut two pieces of cheesecloth, each measuring 4½ x 5½ inches. Cut embroidered netting to match, and baste to each piece of cheesecloth. Place right sides together, pin and stitch, leaving an opening. Trim the seam and turn, then fill with potpourri and slipstitch the opening. Use two 27½-inch lengths of ribbon to tie the cheesecloth up like a parcel.

LAVENDER BOTTLES

"Bottles" of long-stemmed lavender, woven with ribbons, will scent all your linen beautifully. Layer the bottles between the sheets in your linen closet or cupboard, or hang them anywhere their delicate fragrance will be appreciated.

Choose lavender with long stalks and pick approximately fifteen stems, making sure that they are all similar in thickness and length. Harvest the lavender when it is ripe and at a time of day when any dew will have dried.

Tie the lavender stalks together just under the heads, with one end of an 80-inch length of ⅛-inch-wide ribbon. Bend the stalks back on themselves and fan them out around the heads to create enough space for weaving the ribbon. Next, thread the longer ribbon end into a blunt tapestry needle, and use this to weave the

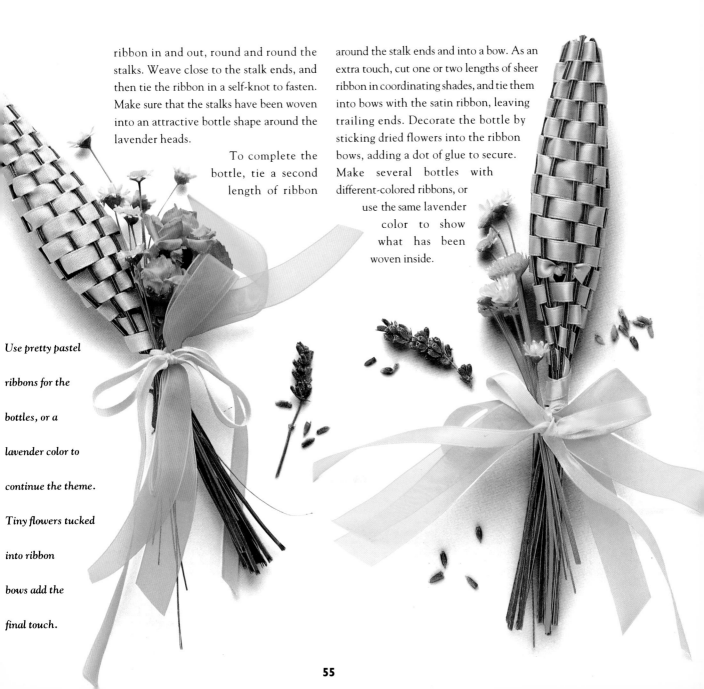

ribbon in and out, round and round the stalks. Weave close to the stalk ends, and then tie the ribbon in a self-knot to fasten. Make sure that the stalks have been woven into an attractive bottle shape around the lavender heads.

To complete the bottle, tie a second length of ribbon around the stalk ends and into a bow. As an extra touch, cut one or two lengths of sheer ribbon in coordinating shades, and tie them into bows with the satin ribbon, leaving trailing ends. Decorate the bottle by sticking dried flowers into the ribbon bows, adding a dot of glue to secure. Make several bottles with different-colored ribbons, or use the same lavender color to show what has been woven inside.

Use pretty pastel ribbons for the bottles, or a lavender color to continue the theme. Tiny flowers tucked into ribbon bows add the final touch.

STUNNING STOCKINGS

Get into the Christmas spirit with these delightful felt stockings. Each

one uses glittery ribbons for the decoration and is very simple to put

together. Make a loop at the back and hang the stocking on the

mantelpiece – all ready for Santa's presents!

Draw a pattern for a stocking 16 inches long and 6½ inches wide, copying the shape of a sock or a picture. When the stocking looks realistic, cut out the pattern, and then use it to cut out two stocking pieces from felt.

To make the first stocking, cut two Christmas ribbons into lengths, lay them alternately and diagonally across one stocking piece, and pin and topstitch them in position. Place the stocking pieces with right sides facing, and pin and stitch them together all around, leaving the top edge open. Turn right side out. Make a loop from ribbon and sew it to the

Alternating ribbon

in diagonal stripes,

with a lavish gold

bow around the top,

makes an attractive

design (left).

together, and stitch the side seams. Stitch lace ribbon around the lower edge of the cuff, and then stitch another length of ribbon just above this.

With the right sides facing, stitch the stocking pieces together and turn them right side out. Stitch a ribbon loop to the back of the stocking to hang it up. With the right side of the cuff to the wrong side of the stocking, pin and then stitch the cuff in place and turn it right side out.

Brightly colored

ribbons with lace

trim decorate the

cuff on this stocking.

Filled with little

presents, it will

give any child

a wonderful

surprise on

Christmas

morning.

back of the stocking to hang it up.

Stitch a piece of gold lamé ribbon along the center of 1½-inch-wide grosgrain ribbon, and then stitch this around the top of the stocking. Make a gold lamé bow and sew this in place to complete the stocking.

For the second stocking, use the same pattern as before to cut two stocking shapes from felt, and also two 5-inch-deep cuffs. Lay some decorative Christmas ribbons over the cuff, and when the arrangement is complete, pin and topstitch them in place.

Position the cuff pieces with right sides

To make the hanging ball shown opposite, cut a 31½-inch length of gold lamé ribbon and fold it in half crosswise. Thread it through the center of a styrofoam ball. Knot the ends together at the base (the rest of the ribbon will form the hanging loop).

Cut 10-inch lengths of the following ribbons: ⅛-inch-wide red-and-gold ribbon, ⅜-inch-wide red-and-green ribbon, ½-inch-wide gold lamé ribbon, 1-inch-wide green-plaid ribbon, and 1-inch-wide red-plaid ribbon.

Fold each length of ribbon into three loops. Bind the centers of the loops with florists' wire, and twist the ends together. Push the ends

CHRISTMAS COLOR

Bring some individuality to Christmas with your own decorations. This hanging bauble and stunning candle holder would add holiday cheer to any table setting.

The beautiful decorations opposite can be made in any color combination to suit your décor and used year after year.

into the styrofoam ball. Wrap wire around the bases of several tiny pine cones, and wind the ends together. Push the ends into different parts of the ball to complete the arrangement.

Make the base of the candle holder by binding a 6-inch-diameter styrofoam ring with ¼-inch-wide green ribbon, overlapping the edges in the center and spreading them out around the outer edge.

Make simple rosettes of green, gold lamé, and red ribbons by working running stitch along one edge of each ribbon and pulling it up (see page 11). Glue the rosettes evenly around the ring. Finally, make some bows from tartan-plaid ribbon, and glue them and a few pine cones and seed pods between the rosettes.

Ribbon loops, bows, and rosettes, interspersed with pine cones and seed pods, create a wonderfully festive feel.

LABOR OF LOVE

Make sure that your message of true love is received loud and clear on February 14 by making your own Valentine. Your card will be totally original, and the traditional red ribbons and heart shapes will show the object of your affection that you really care. Both of the cards shown here are very simple to make, or you could come up with your own variation.

To make the pretty card on the left, cut a piece of cardboard to 18 x 18¼ inches. Score across the cardboard on both sides, 6 inches and 12 inches from one short edge to make three sections (these will fold in a "concertina" shape later to make the finished card shape). Mark a 1-inch border all around the front section of the card, and cut out the center. Take a piece of pink paper measuring 8¼ x 6 inches and glue this to the second section of the card.

Make up four roses using 13¼ inches of ⅜-inch-wide velvet ribbon. Draw the rose stems and leaves on the card, and then glue the roses in place. Make a bow from ⅜-inch-wide heart-print ribbon, and glue it in place. Fold the card. Add decoration around the border with

A homemade ribbon

card, rather than a

purchased one,

makes a really

personal Valentine's

day gift for someone

special.

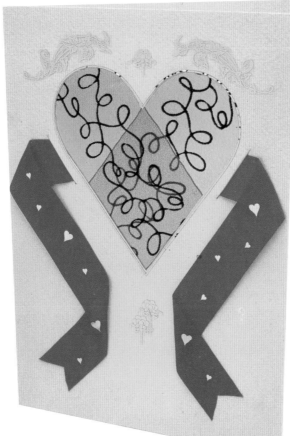

gold pen
or self-adhesive stickers if you wish.

To make the heart card opposite, cut a piece of cardboard to the same size as the roses card, and score it across in the same way. On another piece of paper, draw a heart shape just under the size of the card. To make sure that the heart is symmetrical, fold the heart in half down the center, and then cut around the outer edge. Unfold the paper, place the heart shape on the card, and mark around it carefully. Cut out the heart from the two front sections of

the card, and make a slit on each side of the heart in the front section only.

Glue 2-inch-wide sheer ribbon in place behind the front heart. Thread ¼-inch-wide satin ribbon into the slits, glue on the wrong side to secure, and then fold and glue it in place on the front, as shown. Glue the first and second sections of the card together, and fold it up.

PAPER MAGIC

Paper ribbons come in many different widths and colors, and each variation can be twisted and tied into attractive arrangements. Unwrap and spread out the wide ribbon, and use it to wrap basket handles and boxes. Pull the thinner craft ribbon against scissor blades to make it curl and wave in wonderful ways.

Paper ribbon makes beautiful ties for gift wrapping. Here, cream and ivy-colored ribbons, combined with plain brown paper, create a lovely natural feel.

Packages wrapped in ordinary brown paper look stunning when decorated with paper ribbon in harmonizing colors. To decorate the round box, unravel the paper ribbon and make two bows – the larger one from green ribbon, and the smaller one from cream ribbon. Lay the cream bow on top of the green one and bind the center with a small band of green ribbon. Glue the bows to the center of the box top and decorate it with nuts to complete the rustic effect.

The decoration on the square box is also very simple. Wrap once around the box with a strip of green ribbon. Tie the ends of the ribbon

Simple paper-ribbon

flowers adorn the

top of this pretty

wreath, with more

ribbon wrapped

around it and

flowers tucked

inside.

together, and then unravel the center section of each end piece, leaving the ends tightly twisted to create a "leaf" shape. Tie a length of cream ribbon at right angles to the green ribbon, and unravel the centers of the end sections in the same way.

The wreath shown above would look attractive in any kitchen. To make it, first wind a basic cane wreath with narrow craft paper ribbon. Work diagonally around the wreath once, and then go around again, overlapping the previous ribbon in a criss-cross fashion. Tie lengths of the same ribbon around the bound ribbons at intervals, and curl the ends by pulling a scissor blade along them.

Make two paper flowers by cutting out petal shapes from unraveled paper ribbon. Bind the petals together around short lengths of tightly twisted ribbon to form stamens. Glue in beads to make the centers, and glue the flowers to the top of the wreath. Glue on pine cones and nuts, and weave in random flowers as you wish.

ACKNOWLEDGMENTS

The author would like to thank the following for their help with the ribbon projects:
Caroline Birkett-Harris, Penny Hill, Beryl Miller, and Pamela Westland.

Quarto would also like to thank the following for kindly providing ribbons for the
projects in this book:

Mokuba Co., Ltd, 4-16-8 Kuramae, Taito-ku, Tokyo, Japan. Phone: 81-3-3864-7700.
Fax: 81-3-3864-4013.
C.M. Offray & Son Ltd. Phone: (908)-879-4700.
Panda ribbons from *Selectus Ltd*, Biddulph, Stoke-on-Trent ST8 7RH, United Kingdom.
Phone: 782-522316.